JINGLE BELL *Rhapsody*

ARRANGED FOR ORGAN BY

Grimoaldo Macchia

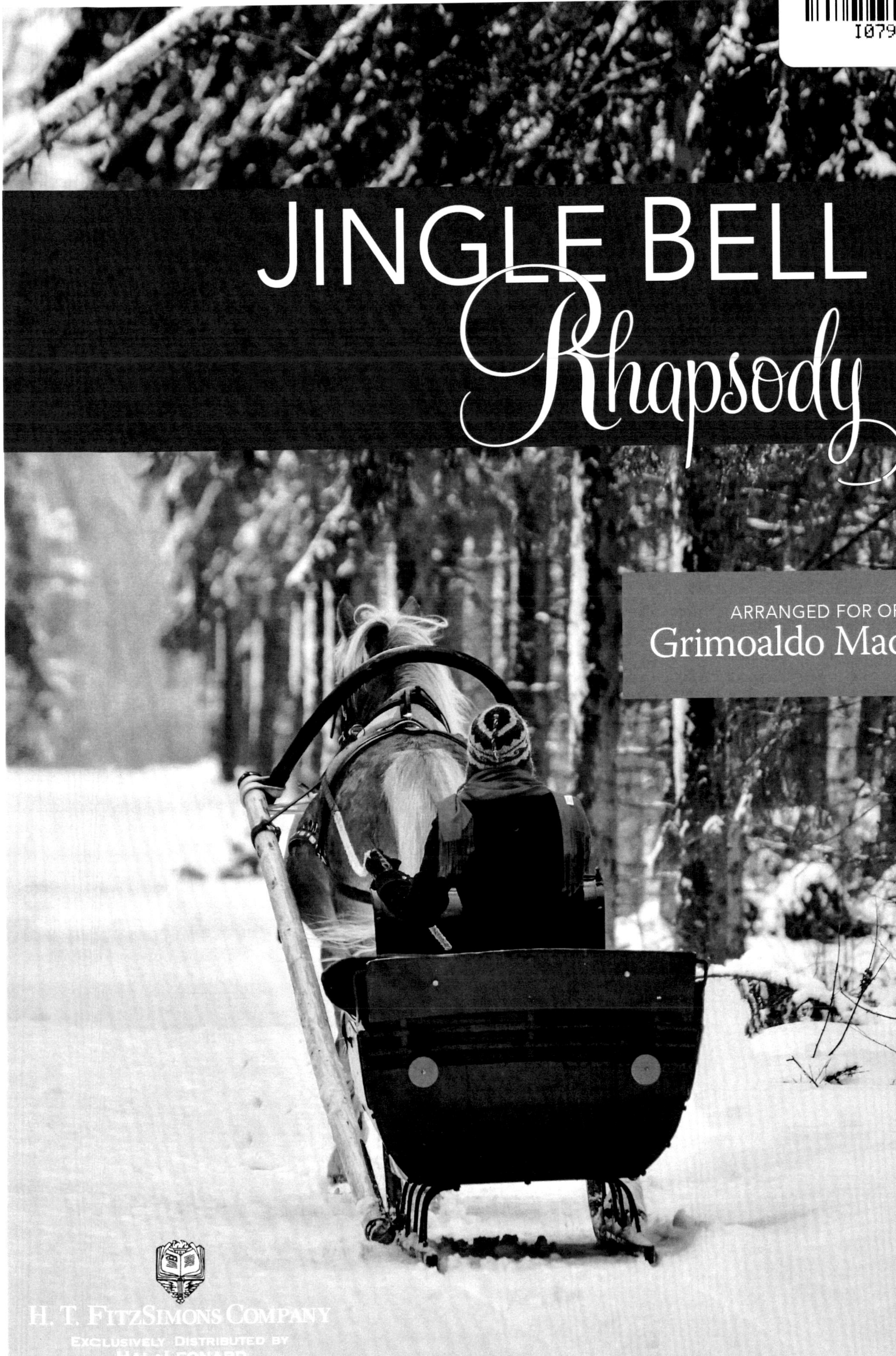

H. T. FitzSimons Company
Exclusively Distributed by
Hal•Leonard

For my friend, Marko Hakanpää

Jingle Bells Rhapsody

J. Pierpoint
Arr. by Grimoaldo Macchia

12
mf
Solo Clarinet
Vox
Cel.
p
Declamato
15
Bells
Vox
Cel.
mp
Glockenspiel or Fl. 8' +Larigot
8va
21
(8va)
26
tr
poco rit.

Moderate swing ♩. = ca. 116
30
Diapasons 8', 4' (Trem.)
simulating a Hammond
mf
marcato
33
36
39

42
45
48
Solo Trumpet
51

54
57
Principal 8'
Solo Trumpet
60
63
tr
f

Valzer giocoso e leggiero
66
Harm.
Fl. 8'
mp
p
72
77
82
Glockenspiel
mp

Principal 8'
mf

109
Solo Trumpet
Principal 8'
114
8va
Glockenspiel or Fl. 8' +Larigot
Jubilant
+ Reeds
fff
119
123

Sw. Full,
Gt. Full, Sw. to Gt.
Ped. Full, Reeds 16', 8'
Toccata
127
Sw. f staccato
130
133
poco rit.
Gt. a tempo ff
136

139
141
143
rit.
146
Fugue
Gt.
(+ Reeds)

149
152
155
157
(+ Reeds)
f
159

161
163
165
167

169
172
Ch. Light echo
Gt.
f
175
Ch.
Gt.
Ch.
178
Gt.

181
ff
183
185
188
molto rit.

Alla marcia
190
Sw.
+ Reeds
fff
193
Solo Trumpet
ff
Prin. 8', 4', 2'
ffff
198
202
fff
+ Reeds
Gt.
Tutti
ffff
gliss.